Color each pair of matching stock

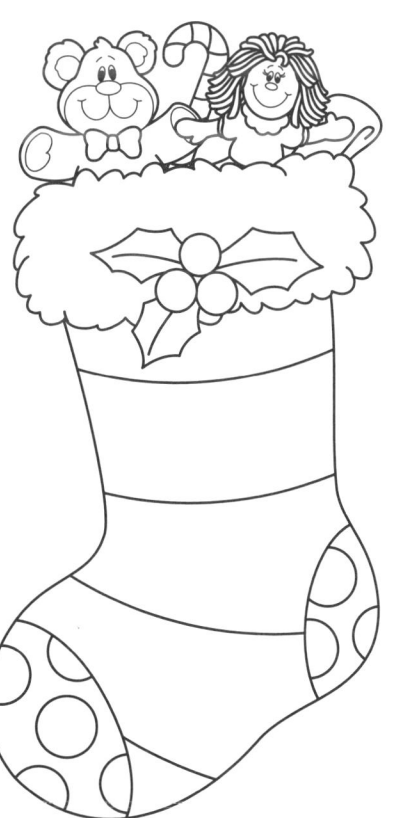
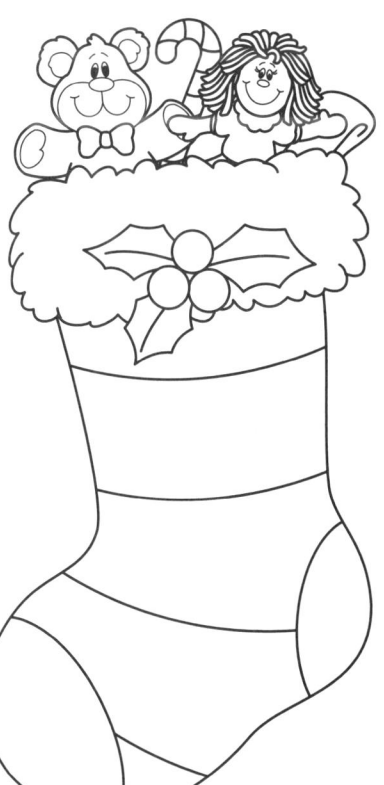

Color by number to see a Christmas flower.

1 = yellow   2 = red   3 = blue   4 = green

Find and circle the holiday words from the word list.

Word List

BELLS
CANDLE
ELF
GIFT
HOLLY
LIGHTS
SLEIGH
STOCKING
TOYS
TREE

```
B E L L S H S V B G
S H M H O L L Y P S
T R E E D F T Z B L
O R F W O U O S Y E
C T R O K T Y M C I
K J O S J H S V B G
I Q M C G I F T Y H
N S N I X D N N E O
G L V I Z I I V Q P
E L F M Q E N S I V
T E E Y L I G H T S
C A N D L E Y M F I
```

Decorate your tree and wrap your gifts with these fun and easy projects.

Christmas Chain

1. Cut red, white, and green paper into several 3" x 6" rectangles.
2. Fold each in half lengthwise and cut a smaller rectangle out of the center, leaving a rectangular frame (figures 1 and 2).
3. To assemble, unfold one frame and push through the opening in another (figure 3). Fold over to connect chain links (figure 4).
4. Continue until chain is desired length.

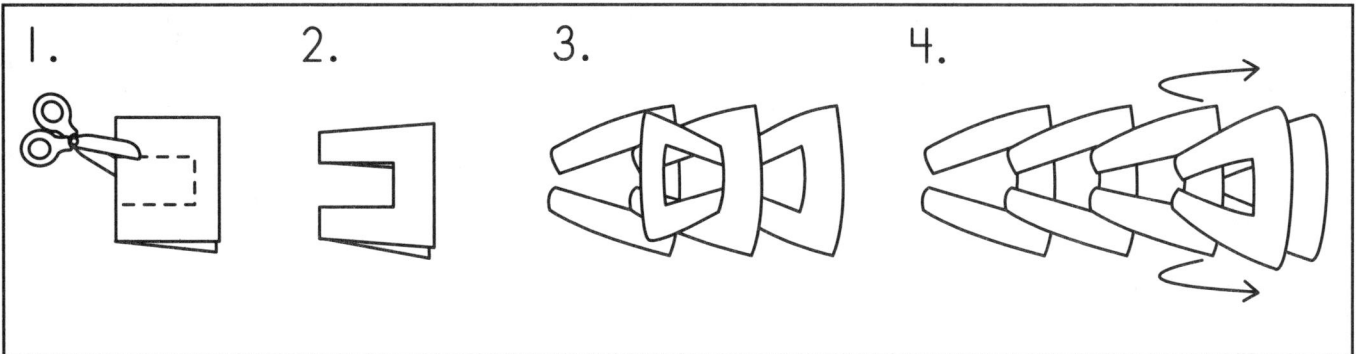

Handy Wrapping Paper

1. Cut down one seam of a paper grocery bag, cut out the bottom, and lay the paper flat.
2. Dip your hands in red and green finger paint, and make handprints on the paper.
3. Let the paper dry before using.

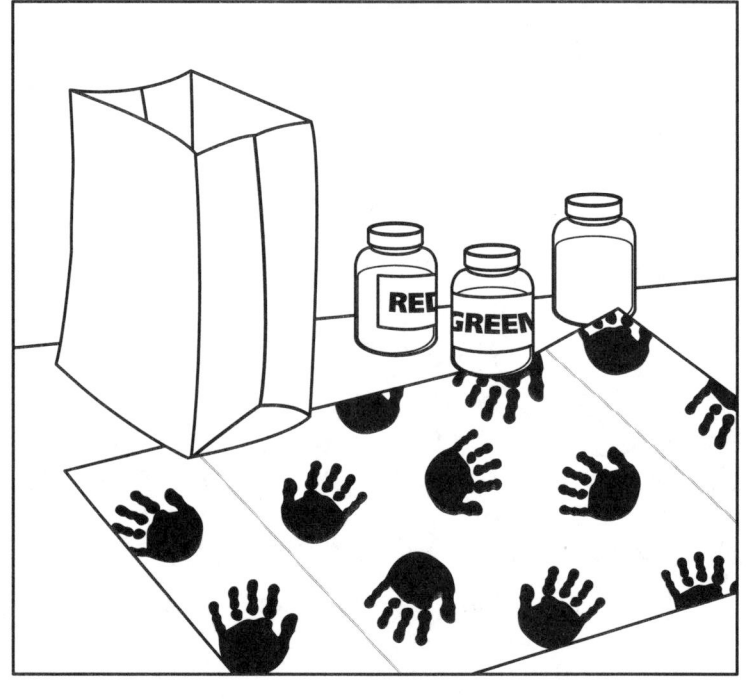

Make a pretty Christmas tree decoration.

1. Color. Cut out the tree on the heavy lines.
2. Fold the tree on the dashed lines.
3. Tape the sides together along the tab to form a pyramid.
4. Stand the tree on a table as a centerpiece.

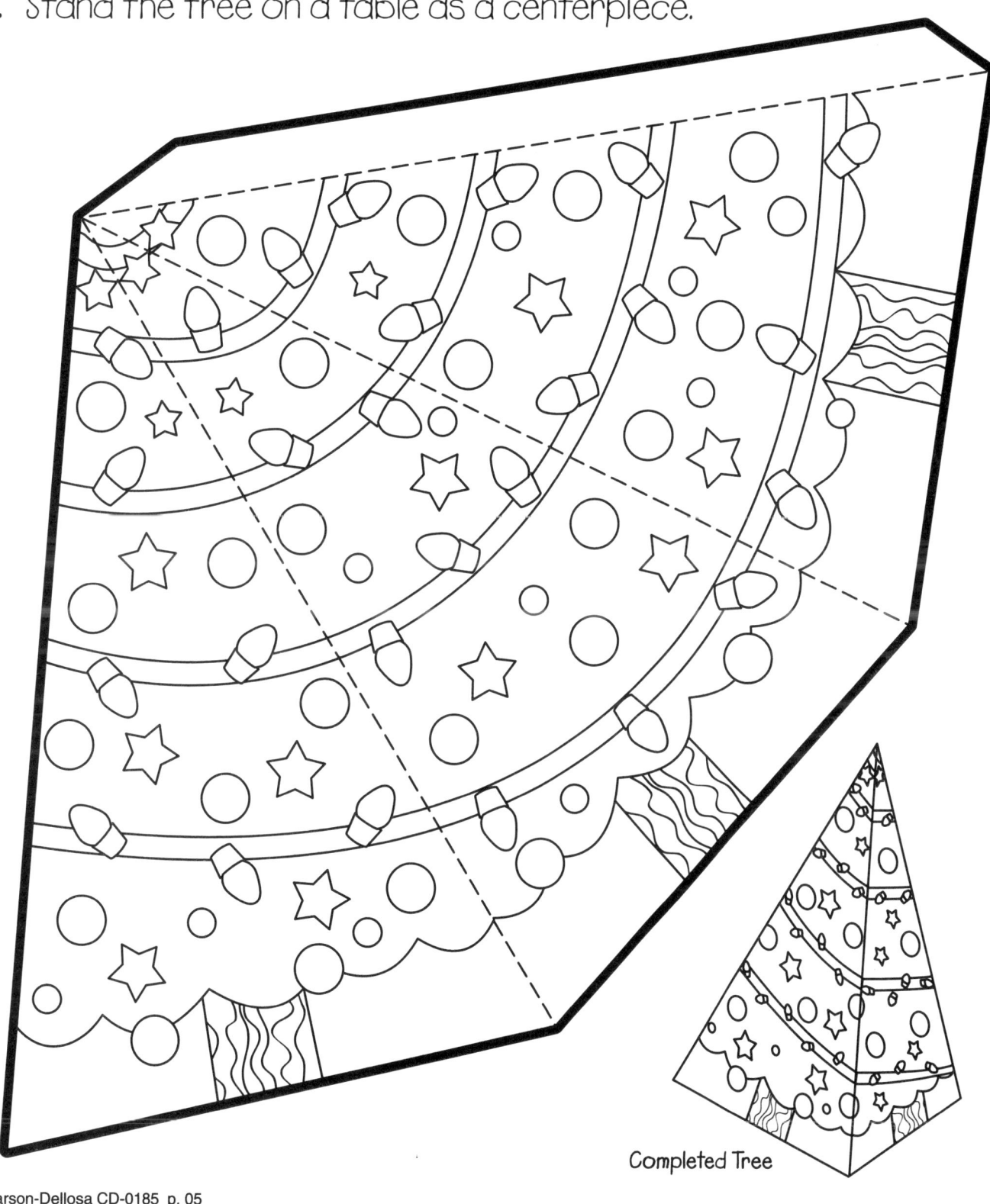

Completed Tree

Help the mouse find his way through the stocking.

Start

Finish

Use the word list to solve the crossword puzzle.

Word List
BELLS
BOWS
CAROLS
COOKIES
RED
ROOFTOP
STAR

Across
1. Christmas songs
4. Up on the _____
5. These jingle on Santa's reindeer
6. A traditional Christmas color

Down
1. Food we decorate with colored sugar and icing
2. Ribbon decorations for packages
3. Decorates the top of the Christmas tree

Connect the dots to complete the picture. Start at the ★.

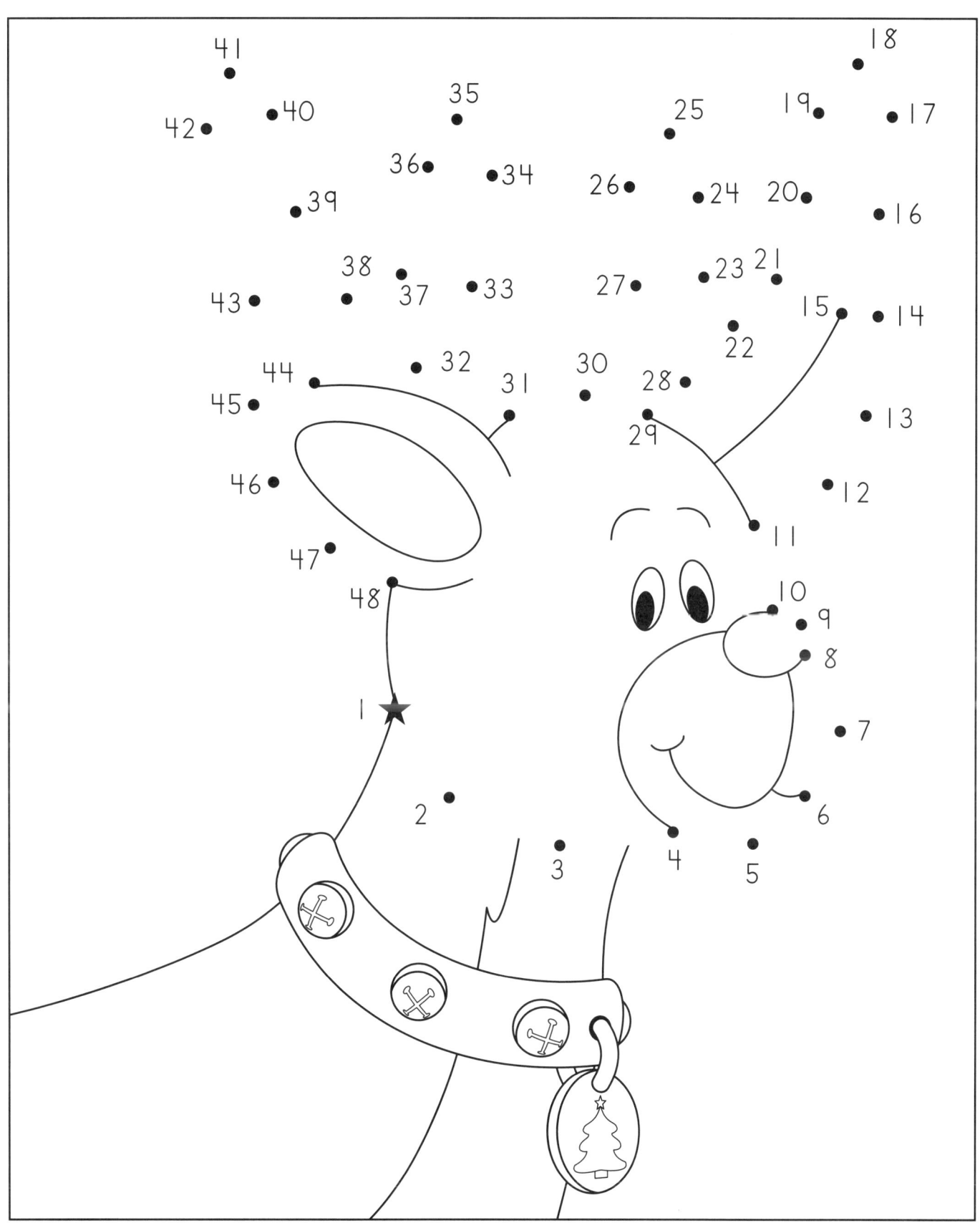

Make candy cane cookies to eat or hang on the Christmas tree!

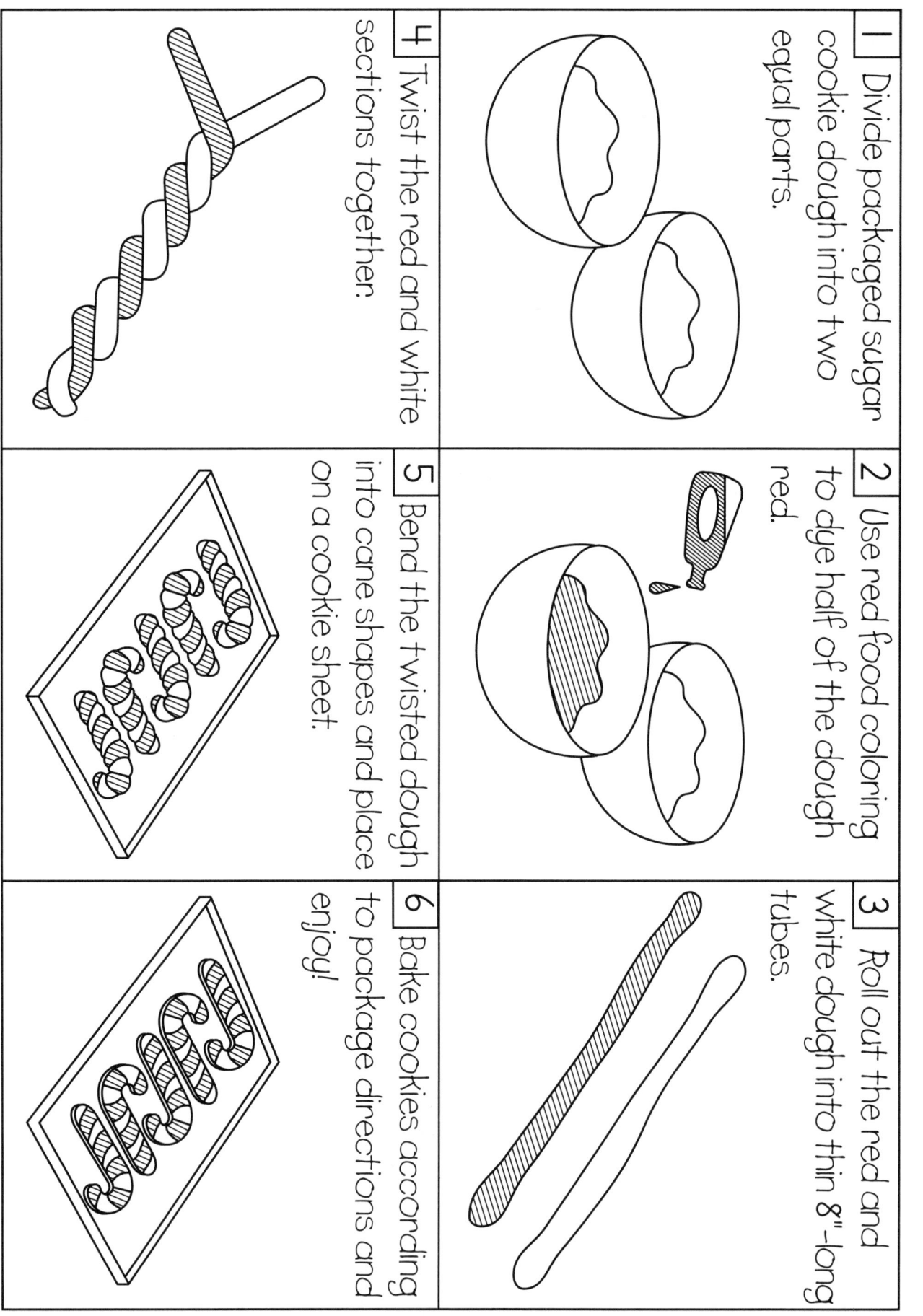

1. Divide packaged sugar cookie dough into two equal parts.

2. Use red food coloring to dye half of the dough red.

3. Roll out the red and white dough into thin 8"-long tubes.

4. Twist the red and white sections together.

5. Bend the twisted dough into cane shapes and place on a cookie sheet.

6. Bake cookies according to package directions and enjoy!

Make this snowman flip book.

1. Cut out each page of the book on the heavy lines.
2. Stack the pages with page 1 on top and staple along left side.
3. Hold the book in your left hand, flip the pages from front to back with your right thumb, and watch him melt away!

Find and circle these hidden objects in the picture: gift, wreath, stocking, Christmas tree, ornament, candy cane, Christmas light, bell, candle, and star. Color the picture.

Use the secret code to answer the questions.

What do you call a deer in a thunderstorm?

" _____ "

___ ___ ___ ___ ___ ___ ___ ___ ___

Where does Frosty the Snowman keep his money?

___ ___ ___ ___ ___ ___ ___

___ ___ ___ ___

What did the gingerbread man put on his bed?

___ ___ ___ ___ ___ ___ ___

___ ___ ___ ___ ___

Gather some friends and play these fun games!

Christmas Carol Tag

Choose two "Its" to try to tag other players. The "Its" must hold their hands on their heads like antlers. When someone is tagged, she also becomes an "It." You can be safe from being tagged by stopping in place and singing a Christmas song.

Stocking Relay

Divide into equal teams and give everyone a stocking. The first person in each group will fill his stocking with 10–15 small items. Then, he will pass the stocking to the next person on his team. She will unpack the first stocking and fill her stocking. Continue unpacking and filling until everyone on the team has filled his stocking. The first group to finish wins.

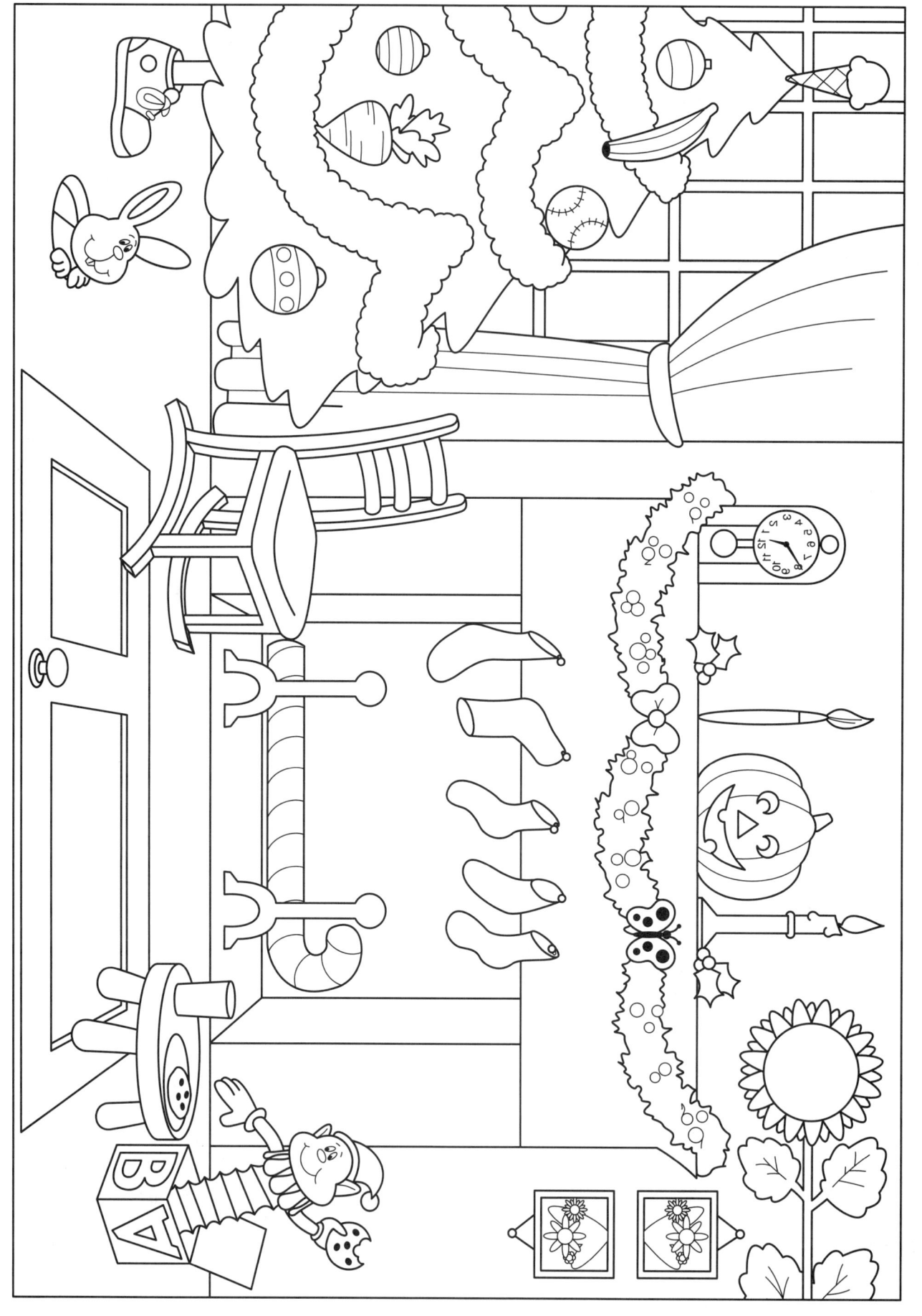

Find and circle 18 things wrong in the picture. Color the picture.

Write Santa a thank-you note for your Christmas gifts. Color the card. Cut it out on the heavy line. On the back, write a thank-you note and sign your name. Fold on the dashed lines and seal with tape or glue.

From: _____

_____

_____

North Pole

Santa Claus
8 Reindeer Way
North Pole

Glue or
tape seal here.

Unscramble the words and circle them in the puzzle.

HTWREA _____

YLIADHO _____

TRSA _____

TNNAMREO _____

YMNCHIE _____

REERENDI _____

TPRSEESN _____

TNSRDECOIAO _____

LROAC _____

VSELE _____

RACDS _____

ECALDN _____

GJILEN _____

YLJOL _____

LBSEL _____

```
D B R E I N D E E R S
C E E J I N G L E D T
J A C L P A C Z R N R
C W R O L T F A E J C
H R C O R S C M K O A
I E E I L A A L N L N
M A X C S N T S N L D
N T M E R W O I T Y L
E H V O S N B E O A E
Y L H O L I D A Y N R
E K P R E S E N T S S
```

SANTA

How many words can you make from the letters in this word?

ORNAMENTS

1. _____
2. _____
3. _____
4. _____
5. _____
6. _____
7. _____
8. _____
9. _____
10. _____
11. _____
12. _____
13. _____
14. _____
15. _____
16. _____

17. _____
18. _____
19. _____
20. _____
21. _____
22. _____
23. _____
24. _____
25. _____
26. _____
27. _____
28. _____
29. _____
30. _____

Use these puppets to act out holiday stories or plays.

1. Color each puppet and cut out on the heavy lines..
2. Use a sharpened pencil to carefully punch a hole through the centers of both circles at the bottom of each puppet. Use scissors to cut out the remaining portion of the circles.
3. Place your first two fingers through the holes of a puppet to form the legs. Make the puppet move by moving your fingers.
4. Make up your own stories for the puppets, or use the story starters on the back of this page.

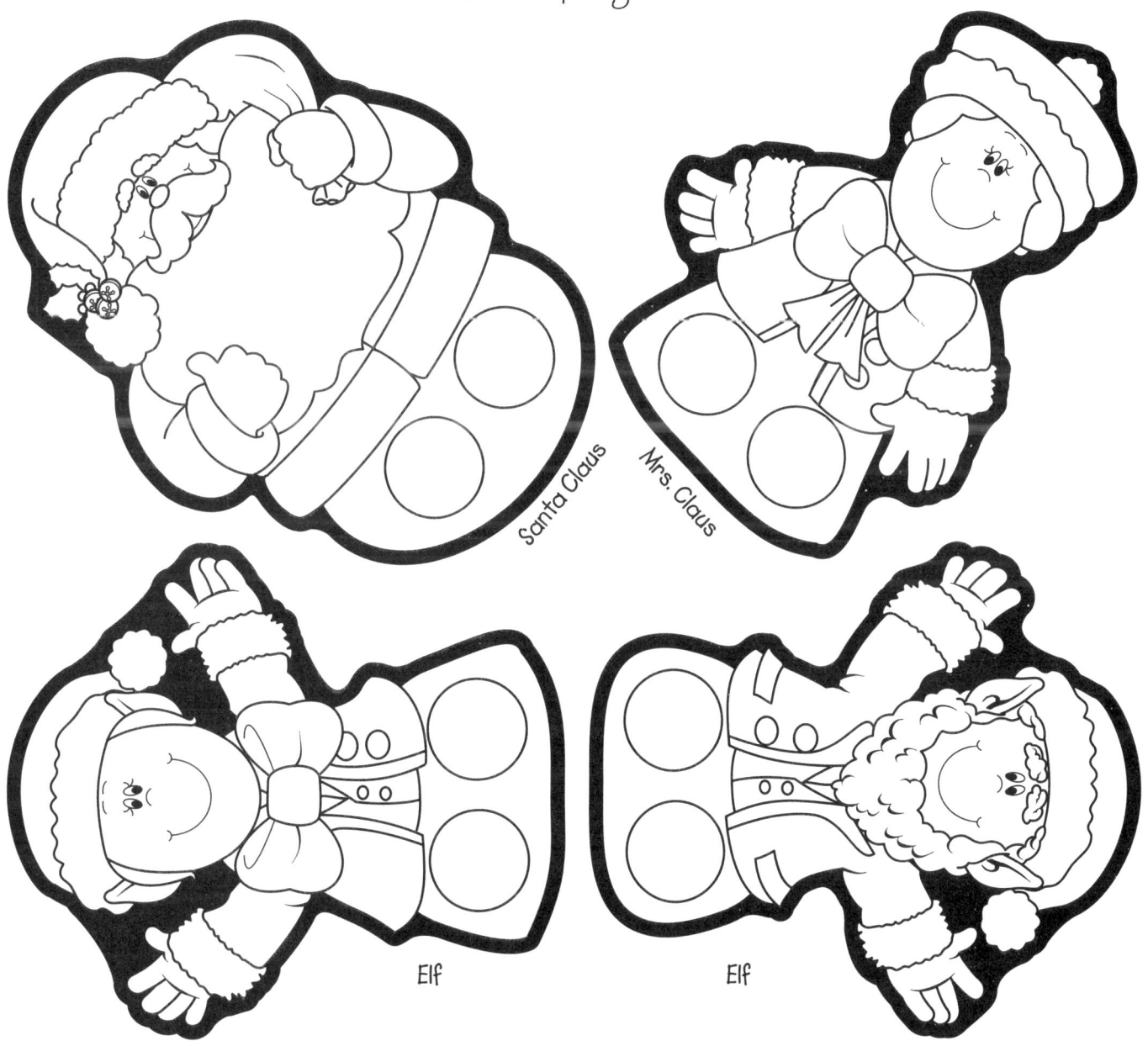

Santa Claus

Mrs. Claus

Elf

Elf

Use these story starters with the puppets on page 21, or make up your own stories.

1. Santa is worried that all of the toys won't be made by Christmas Eve.
2. This year Mrs. Claus decided she wants to drive the sleigh on Christmas Eve.
3. Santa's elves have a big surprise for Santa and Mrs. Claus.
4. It is Christmas day, all of the toys are delivered, and Santa, Mrs. Claus, and the elves are having a big Christmas party.

Color the picture of Santa putting gifts under the tree.

Help the elf find his way through Santa's workshop to the sleigh. Color the picture.

Start

Finish

Make a candle. Shine a flashlight on the completed candle and watch it sparkle.

1. Decorate a cardboard tube, and cut two 1" slits on opposite sides of one end.
2. Cut out the candle flame and glow patterns. Color and add glitter. (If making more than one candle, copy the patterns first.)
3. Glue the flame to the inside edge of the candle glow.
4. Slide flame into the slits.
5. Make several candles from different-sized tubes to make a candle grouping.

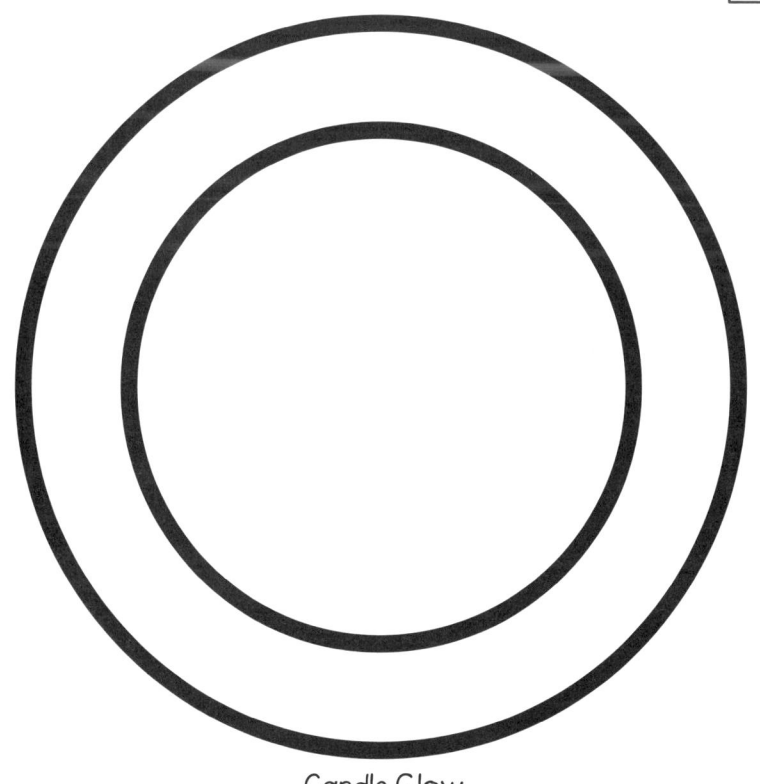

Candle Glow

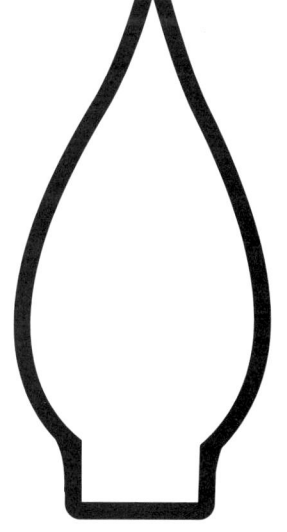

Candle Flame

Decorate with these homemade crafts.

Gingerbread House

1. Staple the top of a clean, pint-sized milk carton closed, and secure it to a heavy-duty paper plate with icing. (See recipe below.)
2. Cover the outsides of the carton with icing.
3. Press graham cracker sections into the icing to resemble a miniature gingerbread house.
4. Decorate the house with candies, such as gumdrops, candy dots, and peppermints. Use icing to "glue" on the candies.

Icing Recipe

3 cups confectioners' sugar
$1/4$ teaspoon cream of tartar
2 egg whites, beaten

Handprint Wreath

1. Trace your hand about 10 times on green construction paper.
2. Cut out the handprints.
3. Glue the handprints together in a wreath shape with the wrists overlapping. If desired, curl the fingers.
4. Glue on a red ribbon bow or make one from red construction paper.

Use the word list to solve the crossword puzzle.

Across

2. Christmas tree decorations
7. A Christmas flower
8. Where Santa makes his toys
9. What Santa rides in
10. An evergreen with red berries

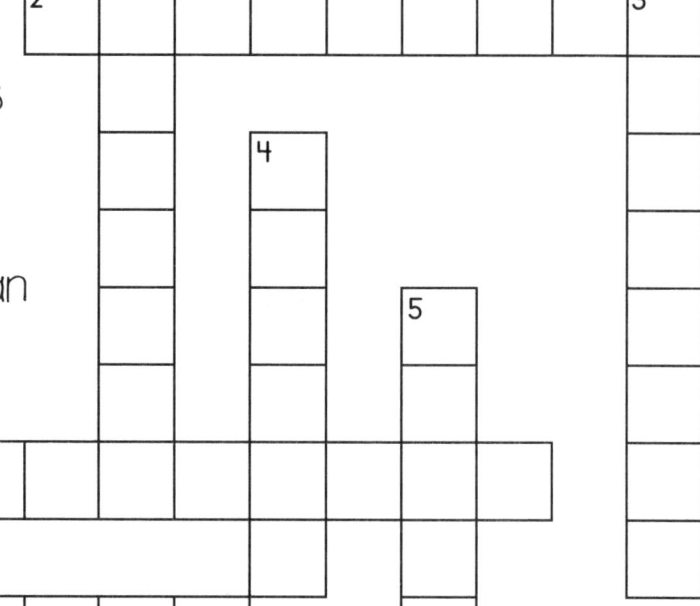

Word List

COOKIES	PRESENTS
FROSTY	REINDEER
HOLLY	SLEIGH
ORNAMENTS	STOCKING
POINSETTIA	WORKSHOP
WREATH	

Down

1. Another name for gifts
3. Hang this on a fireplace
4. Famous snowman
5. Eight of these pull Santa's sleigh
6. Food we leave for Santa
8. A decorative ring that can be hung on doors

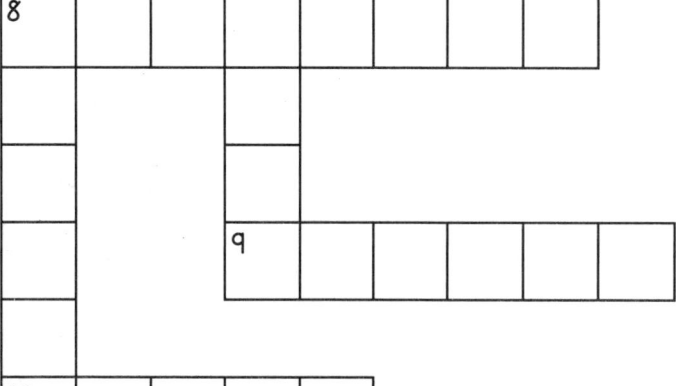

© Carson-Dellosa CD-0185 p. 28

Make this folded box for a special Christmas gift.

1. Color the box.

2. Cut out the box on the heavy lines.

3. Fold the box and tabs on the lines shown below.

4. Glue or tape tabs to inside of box. Do not glue lid closed.

5. Place gift inside box and close lid.

Color and cut out the gift tags to tie or tape to gifts.

To:

From:

To:

From:

To:

From:

To:

From:

To:

From:

To:

From:

To:

From:

To:

From: